table for two
french recipes
for romantic dining

Translated from the French by Louise Guiney

Copyediting: Susan Kennedy

Design: Maud Allenet

Typesetting: Anne-Lou Bissières

Proofreading: B. Fernandez

Color separation: Penez Édition, Lille

Originally published as *La Cuisine des Amoureux*
© Éditions Flammarion, 2002
English-language edition © Éditions Flammarion, 2003

04 05 06 5 4 3 2

FC0419-04-I
ISBN: 2-0803-0419-4
Dépôt legal: 01/2004

Printed in Spain

table for two
french recipes
for romantic dining

Marianne Paquin

Photographs
Jacques Boulay

Contents

Introduction

Influence of Gourmandism
upon Conjugal Happiness

by Brillat-Savarin*
(1755–1826)

"Finally, gourmandism, when it is shared, has the most marked influence upon the happiness attainable in the married state.

Let the twain be gourmands, and at least once a day they have the occasion to enjoy each other's company; for even those who sleep apart (and there are many such) eat at the same table; they have a theme of conversation which never grows stale, for they talk not only of what they are eating, but of what they are about to eat, what they have met with on the tables of their acquaintances, fashionable dishes, new inventions, etc., etc., and such table-talk is full of charm. [. . .]

A common need calls man and wife to table, and the same inclination keeps them there; they are naturally attentive to each other, and show, by their courtesy, a mutual wish to please; the manner in which meals are conducted is an important ingredient in the happiness of life.

This last piece of wisdom, which is new to France, did not

escape the English moralist, Richardson; he enlarges upon it in his novel *Pamela*, where he describes the different way in which two married couples end their day.

The two husbands are brothers; one, the elder, is a peer enjoying full possession of the family estate; the other, and younger, is the husband of Pamela, disinherited on account of his marriage, and living upon the proceeds of his half-pay in circumstances not far removed from poverty.

The peer and his lady enter their dining-room from opposite doors, and greet each other coldly, although it is their first meeting of the day. They sit down to a lavishly spread table, surrounded by lackeys gleaming with gold; they are served in dead silence, and without zest. However, when the servants withdraw, a kind of conversation ensues between them; but soon restraint breaks down; she turns shrewish, and the pair rise from the table infuriated, to seek separate rooms, where each meditates the sweets of the widowed state.

The younger brother, on the contrary, upon reaching his humble lodging, is welcomed with tender effusion and the softest of caresses. He sits down to a frugal board; but the excellence of his meal is none the less assured, for has not Pamela herself prepared it? They eat with unfeigned delight, talking meanwhile of their affairs, their projects and their love. A half bottle of Madeira serves to prolong both meal and talk; and then one bed receives them, and sweet sleep crowns the bliss of mutual love, bringing forgetfulness of the present and dreams of better days to come.

All honor then to gourmandism [. . .]!"

* Anthelme Brillat-Savarin, writer, magistrate, and gourmand, is known, above all, for his extended essay on gastronomy: *The Physiology of Taste or Meditations on Transcendental Gastronomy* (1825) from which the above extract is taken. This essay was originally published in French by Champs Flammarion. The translation here is taken from the 1925 English-language edition published by Peter Davies, Ltd. and Doubleday and Company, London and New York.

Cocooning

In winter treat yourself to structured, generous,
full-bodied wines—Bordeaux, Saint-Émilion,
Australian, and Chilean vintages.

16

Mushroom soup with coconut

Ingredients

- *7 oz. (200 g) white mushrooms*
- *1 shallot*
- *2 tablespoons butter*
- *¼ chicken bouillon cube*
- *salt, pepper*
- *1 small can unsweetened coconut milk*
- *½ bunch fresh coriander*

Clean the mushrooms, removing the stems, and slice. Peel and chop the shallot and gently sauté in the butter for 2 minutes. Add the mushrooms and sauté 5 minutes longer. Make a bouillon by dissolving the cube in ½ cup of boiling water, then pour over the mushrooms and cook for 5 minutes to reduce the liquid, stirring all the time. Season with salt and pepper, add ¾ cup (20 cl) coconut milk, and reduce over a low heat for 7–8 minutes more. Chop the coriander and garnish the soup before serving.

Canned coconut milk is readily available at Asian grocery stores and supermarkets.

Upside-down turnip tarts with sautéed foie gras

Ingredients

- 6 small turnips
- 3 tablespoons butter
- 1 tablespoon granulated sugar
- ½ teaspoon paprika
- ½ teaspoon mixture of pepper, nutmeg, cinnamon, and ginger
- 1 packet ready-to-cook pastry
- 2 slices uncooked foie gras (fresh or canned)
- 1 tablespoon flour
- salt, pepper

Preheat oven to 350°F (180°C).

Wash, pare, and quarter the turnips, then sauté them gently in 2 tablespoons butter and ½ tablespoon granulated sugar for 15 minutes. Stir in the paprika and the other spices. Use the remaining butter to grease two small, non stick tart molds. Sprinkle with the remaining sugar and fill the molds evenly with the turnip quarters. Roll out the pastry, cut it into two disks the same diameter as the molds, and place on top of the turnips. Bake for 15–20 minutes, or until golden. Turn the tarts out onto individual serving dishes: when you carefully lift off the mold the turnips should be on top and the pastry at the bottom. Dredge the slices of raw liver with flour and sauté 30 seconds on each side in a very hot, ungreased frying pan. Season with salt and pepper, arrange on top of the tarts, and serve immediately.

You can use small, ready-to-cook turnips available in the frozen-food section of most supermarkets for this recipe.

Salad with goat cheese and dried figs

Ingredients

- 1 small head lettuce
- 2 tablespoons sunflower oil
- 1 tablespoon cider vinegar
- salt, pepper
- 1 teaspoon sesame seeds
- 2 slices country bread
- 4 dried figs
- 1 small St. Marcellin goat cheese

Trim, wash, and drain the lettuce. Toss the leaves in a vinaigrette made with the oil, vinegar, salt and pepper. Brown the sesame seeds in a frying pan. Toast the bread. Cut the figs into thin slices and arrange on the toast; slice the cheese in two horizontal pieces and place on top of the figs. Grill for 2–3 minutes under the broiler, checking frequently. Sprinkle the cheese with sesame seeds and serve on the salad.

St. Marcellin is the best goat cheese for this recipe. It is a very soft cheese, so make sure to select one that is firm and compact for grilling. Use another good-quality creamy goat cheese if St. Marcellin is unavailable.

Beef-on-a-string with horseradish cream

Ingredients

- ¾ cup (20 cl) heavy cream
- a few drops lemon juice
- ½ teaspoon horseradish
- 2 carrots
- 1 leek (white portion only)
- 1 small onion studded with 2 cloves
- 1 bouquet garni
- 1 tablespoon coarse salt
- 1½ teaspoon black pepper
- 1 lb. (450 g) fillet of beef, tied into a compact piece
- 2 pinches pepper

Place the cream and lemon juice in a bowl, whip until firm. Add the horseradish, season with pepper. Chill in the refrigerator until serving time. Pare the carrots, trim the leeks, and cut the vegetables into quarters. Fill a large pot with water and bring to a boil. Add the carrots and leeks, the onion studded with cloves, the bouquet garni, salt and pepper. Tie the fillet of beef with a length of string to a wooden spoon and place the spoon across the top of the pot so that the meat is submerged in the water but does not touch the bottom of the pot. Return the contents to a boil, reduce to simmer, and cook for 15 minutes. Lift out the meat and keep warm on a serving dish. Drain the vegetables and arrange around the meat. Cut the meat into slices and serve accompanied with the vegetables and horseradish cream.

When whipping cream, the bowl and cream should both be well chilled beforehand.

Chicken breasts with chanterelle mushrooms and wild rice

22

Ingredients

- *2 sprigs parsley*
- *1 shallot*
- *2 tablespoons wild rice*
- *2 chicken breasts*
- *¼ lb. (100 g) chanterelle mushrooms*
- *2 tablespoons butter*
- *salt, pepper*
- *2 tablespoons olive oil*

Wash, drain, and chop the parsley. Peel and chop the shallot. Cook the wild rice according to the directions on the packet and drain. Using a sharp knife, cut pockets in the chicken breasts and set aside. Wipe the mushrooms and gently sauté with the shallots in the butter in a frying pan for 3 minutes. Stir into the cooked rice, add the chopped parsley, and season with salt and pepper. Fill the pockets you have made in the chicken breasts with this mixture, and secure them with a toothpick. Heat the olive oil in a frying pan, and cook the chicken breasts, covered, for about 7 minutes on each side. Serve with a green salad.

If fresh chanterelle mushrooms are unavailable, you can replace them with dried mushrooms or canned gourmet "forest" mushrooms.

Stuffed fillet of cod

25

Preheat oven to 350°F (180°C).

Peel and chop the onion, sauté in the olive oil for a few minutes. Pour boiling water over the tomatoes, leave for 1 minute, drain, peel, then remove the seeds, and dice the flesh. Cut the anchovies into small pieces and combine with the chopped onion, diced tomatoes, and capers. Add the thyme leaves after removing the stalk. Season with pepper. Place one cod fillet (skin-side down) in an ovenproof pan. Spread the stuffing mixture over it and cover with the second fillet (skin-side up). Roll the stuffed fillets into a cylinder, as for a rolled roast, and tie securely. Sprinkle with olive oil and bake 20 minutes. Serve immediately. As an optional extra, surround the rolled cod fillets with thin slices of potato before placing the pan in the oven.

Ingredients

- *1 mild onion*
- *2 tablespoons olive oil*
- *2 tomatoes*
- *4 anchovy fillets in oil*
- *1 teaspoon capers*
- *1 sprig thyme*
- *pepper*
- *2 cod fillets, with the skin on*
- *2 peeled potatoes (optional)*

You can prepare any number of portions of this dish in advance and freeze them in individual plastic bags or containers. Defrost and cook in the oven as needed.

Tagliatelli in cream with walnuts, hazelnuts, pistachios, olives, and Parma ham

Ingredients

- *4 shelled walnuts*
- *8 hazelnuts, shelled and blanched*
- *12 pistachios, shelled*
- *8 green olives, pitted*
- *½ cup (10 cl) heavy cream*
- *2 tablespoons olive oil*
- *salt, pepper*
- *2 slices Parma ham*
- *7 oz. (200 g) fresh tagliatelli*

Combine the walnuts, hazelnuts, pistachios, and olives. Reserve a small amount of this mixture for the garnish and place the rest in a serving bowl. Add the cream and olive oil and season with salt and pepper. Cut the slices of ham into strips. Cook the tagliatelli according to the directions on the packet in a large pot of boiling salted water. Drain. Transfer the hot pasta to the serving bowl, mix the contents well, and garnish with the reserved nut mixture and strips of ham. Serve immediately.

To keep the strands of pasta separate during cooking, try adding a tablespoon of oil to the boiling water.

Arugula salad with lentils, jabugo ham, and mustard dressing

Ingredients

- 1 cup (160 g) lentils
- 2 small garlic cloves, peeled
- 1 sprig thyme
- 1 bay leaf
- 1 teaspoon Dijon mustard
- 1 tablespoon balsamic vinegar
- 2 tablespoons olive oil
- salt, pepper
- 2 slices Spanish jabugo ham
- 2 oz. (60 g) pack of arugula leaves

Rinse the lentils and simmer for 20 minutes in a pot of salted water with the thyme, bay leaf, and 1 garlic clove. When the lentils are cooked, drain, remove the garlic, thyme, and bay leaf, and allow to cool. For the vinaigrette dressing, combine the mustard, balsamic vinegar, olive oil, salt and pepper with 1 tablespoon water and mix together thoroughly. Add the remaining garlic clove. Cut the jabugo ham into strips. Toss the arugula with the cold lentils and add the ham. Remove the garlic from the vinaigrette dressing. Pour the dressing over the salad and serve.

Jabugo ham can be substituted with other cured hams such as bayonne or prosciutto.

28

Spiced compote of winter fruits with meringue

Ingredients

- 2 dessert apples
- juice of ½ lemon
- 2 tablespoons salted butter
- 1 teaspoon granulated sugar
- 1 slice stale gingerbread or 2–3 ginger cookies
- 2 egg whites
- 1 teaspoon confectioners' (icing) sugar

Pare, core, and dice the apples. Moisten with the lemon juice. Melt the butter in a pot over low heat, then add the apples and granulated sugar. Cook the apples for 10 minutes, stirring often, until soft. Grate the gingerbread or crush the ginger cookies with a rolling pin. Beat the egg whites with the confectioners' sugar until firm. Preheat the broiler. Pour the apple compote into a shallow ovenproof dish. Sprinkle with the crumbs of ginger and spread with the beaten egg whites. Place under the broiler (not too close to the heat) and brown for 5 minutes, checking frequently. Serve lukewarm.

This recipe can be made with various kinds of winter fruit, and you can also use dried fruits.

Chocolate truffles with custard sauce

30

Ingredients
- *5 oz. (150 g) bitter chocolate*
- *1 teaspoon milk*
- *2 tablespoons butter*
- *1 egg yolk*
- *1 tablespoon heavy cream*
- *4 tablespoons confectioners' (icing) sugar*
- *1 teaspoon Poire Williams (pear) liqueur*
- *1 tablespoon cocoa*

for the custard sauce
- *2 cups (½ l) milk*
- *5 egg yolks*
- *⅓ cups (100 g) granulated sugar*
- *¼ teaspoon potato flour*
- *½ vanilla bean (pod)*

Begin preparing the truffles more than 3 hours in advance. Break the chocolate into pieces and melt with 1 teaspoon milk in the top of a double boiler. Remove from the heat and add the butter gradually, stirring constantly. Add the egg yolk and cream. Mix together thoroughly. Beat in the sugar and pear liqueur. Chill this mixture in the refrigerator for 2 hours. When thoroughly chilled, use a teaspoon to divide the chocolate paste into small pieces. Roll each piece in the palm of the hand to form small flattened ovals and dredge with the cocoa. Chill until serving time. To prepare the custard sauce scald the milk by heating it to just below boiling point. Mix together the egg yolks, granulated sugar, and potato flour in another pot. Split the vanilla bean, scrape out the seeds, and add, with the bean, to this mixture. Slowly add the scalded milk, stirring constantly with a wire whisk. Place over a low heat and continue stirring until the sauce thickens. Do not allow to boil. Transfer the sauce to a bowl and cool. Remove the vanilla bean. Place the chocolate truffles on shallow dessert plates and surround with the custard sauce.

For this recipe, use good quality chocolate with a high cocoa content, or dipping chocolate.

Soup of citrus fruits flavored with vanilla

33

Using a small serrated knife, peel the citrus fruits above a bowl or on a grooved wooden board to catch all the juice. Cut the fruits across into thin round slices and divide between two wide-rimmed parfait glasses. Split the vanilla bean in half lengthwise, scrape the seeds into a small bowl, and add the fruit juice and honey, stirring all together well. Pour this mixture over the sliced fruit. Garnish each glass with half a vanilla bean and a sprig of fresh mint. Chill and serve with small dessert cookies.

Ingredients

- *1 pink grapefruit*
- *1 orange*
- *1 tangerine*
- *1 vanilla bean (pod)*
- *1 tablespoon liquid honey*
- *2 sprigs fresh mint*

For variety: instead of slicing the citrus fruits into rounds, divide into neat segments, using a sharp knife to take off the pith.

Baked apples in spiced milk

34

Ingredients

- *1 vanilla bean (pod)*
- *⅔ cup (15 cl) milk*
- *1 pinch cinnamon*
- *2 dessert apples*
- *3 teaspoons liquid honey*

Preheat oven to 300°F (150°C).

Split the vanilla bean in half, lengthwise, and scrape the seeds into the milk. Add the cinnamon. Peel the apples and remove the cores. Cut the apples in half, horizontally, and place them cut-side down in a shallow ovenproof dish. Pour around the spiced milk and drizzle the honey over the apples. Bake for 1 hour, basting the apples several times with the milk. Remove from oven and cool. Serve for breakfast with cottage cheese, cream cheese, or berry jam.

For a more attractive appearance, leave the apples whole. But if you do this, be sure you baste them even more frequently.

Coffee-cognac cocktail
with cardamom and cinnamon

36

Ingredients

- *1 stick cinnamon*
- *1 cardamom seed*
- *2 egg yolks*
- *¼ cup (6 cl) strong espresso coffee*
- *¼ cup (6 cl) cognac*
- *½ cup (10 cl) heavy cream*

Grate the cinnamon stick (to give you about ¼ teaspoonful of ground cinnamon) and half the cardamom seed. Place the egg yolks, coffee, and cognac in the top of a double boiler. Heat gently over boiling water, beating constantly, until the mixture is thick and creamy. Add the cream and spices. Serve immediately, and sweeten to taste.

If the preparation seems too thick, thin it with a little milk.

Dinner by Candlelight

Champagne, the traditional accompaniment
to festive occasions, is the ideal partner
for the dishes described in this chapter.

40

Soft-boiled eggs with caviar fingers

Ingredients

- *1 pinch coarse salt*
- *4 very fresh eggs*
- *½ loaf of crusty country bread*
- *2 tablespoons butter*
- *1 small jar (about 2 oz. or 60 g) pressed caviar*
- *salt, pepper*

Fill a small pot with cold water, add a pinch of coarse salt, and bring to a roiling boil. Off the heat, carefully slip the eggs into the water, using a tablespoon to avoid breaking them. Cover the pot tightly and allow to stand for 4 minutes. Cut the bread into fingers and spread evenly with the butter and pressed caviar. When the 4 minutes are up, carefully lift the eggs from the water with a slotted spoon and place in egg cups. The cooked eggs should be creamy and liquid. Serve immediately, accompanied with the caviar fingers.

If you have a little more time, before cooking the eggs use a sharp knife to cut the top off each egg, taking care not to break the shell. Empty the contents into a small pan, add a little crème fraîche and dill, and scramble over a low heat until firm and creamy. Place the empty shells in egg cups and fill each one with the creamy scrambled eggs.

Quick-cooked foie gras terrine
with asparagus and truffles

Ingredients

- *1 small uncooked foie gras weighing approximately 1 lb. (450 g)*
- *1 tablespoon cognac or armagnac*
- *¼ teaspoon salt*
- *½ teaspoon ground white pepper*
- *½ lb. (225 g) green asparagus*
- *3 tablespoons sunflower oil*
- *1 tablespoon wine vinegar*
- *1 teaspoon black truffle shavings, with a little of their juice*
- *salt, pepper*

Separate the lobes of the foie gras. Using a sharp knife, carefully remove the nerves and veins, cutting into the flesh if necessary. Place the foie gras in a shallow dish that can be used in a microwave, moisten with the cognac or armagnac, and season with salt and ground white pepper. Marinate for several hours in the refrigerator, remove, and return to room temperature. Cook in the microwave for 2 minutes, 30 seconds (for an 800–900 watt microwave). Remove from the microwave, cover, and allow to cool. Choose a small, deep terrine dish. Cut a piece of fairly stiff cardboard to fit snugly inside the rim and wrap a covering of aluminum foil or plastic wrap around it. Put the foie gras, with its fat, in the terrine, cover with the cardboard lid, and press down with a heavy weight such as a large unopened can. Do not worry if the fat from the foie gras rises and spills over the cardboard. Chill the terrine, under the weight, in the refrigerator for several hours, or until the fat has congealed. Lift off the weight and remove the cardboard lid. Scrape the congealed fat into a small pot, melt it over a low heat, and pour back into the terrine. Return the terrine to the refrigerator and chill for 3 days. Prepare the dish by trimming the asparagus stalks and cooking them in a pot of boiling salted water for 8 minutes—they should be slightly crunchy. Drain on absorbent paper and allow to cool. Prepare a vinaigrette with the oil, vinegar, salt, pepper, shredded truffle shavings and their juice. Cut even slices of the foie gras and arrange on serving plates and garnish with the asparagus. Moisten with the vinaigrette and serve with slices of toasted country bread. Any remaining foie gras should be covered with plastic wrap to protect it from the air and can be stored for several days in the refrigerator.

For an original touch, substitute port for the cognac, and season with Szechuan pepper.

Oysters and fresh herbs in filo pastry

Preheat oven to 400°F (200°C).

Peel and chop the shallot. Rinse, drain, and chop the herbs. Open the oysters (or have this done for you at the fish shop) and remove from their shells. Squeeze the lemon juice into a bowl, add the shallot, herbs, 3 tablespoons olive oil, salt, pepper, and lastly the oysters. Stir gently to combine. Cut each sheet of filo pastry into 6 equal squares. Using a pastry brush, brush the remaining olive oil over the squares. Place a mound of the oyster-and-herb mixture in the center of each square and roll the pastry around the stuffing as you would a candy wrapper. Twist the ends to close securely and place on a baking sheet covered with ovenproof paper. Bake for 5 minutes in a hot oven. Serve immediately.

Ingredients

- *1 shallot*
- *2 sprigs chervil*
- *2 sprigs basil*
- *2 sprigs mint*
- *a few chives*
- *1 dozen oysters*
- *juice of ½ lemon*
- *4 tablespoons olive oil*
- *salt, pepper*
- *2 large sheets ready-to-cook filo pastry*

If, to save time and effort, you request that the oysters be opened at the shop, make sure the juice remains in the open shells as it will keep the oysters fresh until cooked.

Creamed prawn soup with tandoori spices

Ingredients

- ½ lb. (225 g) cooked prawns
- ½ teaspoon fish bouillon powder
- ¾ cup (20 cl) heavy cream
- ½ teaspoon ground tandoori spices
- 1 pinch chili powder
- dill (optional)
- salt, pepper

Set a few whole cooked prawns aside for the garnish. Shell the remaining prawns, discard the heads. Put the tail meat through a blender. Stir the fish bouillon powder into ½ cup (10 cl) boiling water. Place the blended tail meat in a pot with the bouillon, cream, tandoori spices, salt and pepper. Cook over medium heat for 5 minutes, stirring continually.

Strain the soup through a fine sieve and pour into two soup plates. Garnish with the whole prawns, a sprinkling of chili powder, and dill sprigs, if available. Serve immediately.

You can buy ground tandoori spices at Asian and specialty grocery stores.

Baked scampi with bacon and basil

Ingredients

- 4 potatoes (choose a variety suitable for puréeing)
- 2 tablespoons butter
- ½ bunch broadleaf basil
- 6 slices lean smoked bacon
- 12 cooked scampi
- 2 tablespoons olive oil
- ½ teaspoon kosher salt
- ½ teaspoon crushed mixed peppercorns
- salt, pepper

Cook the potatoes, still in their skins, for 20 minutes in boiling salted water. When cool enough to handle, peel them, add the butter, salt and pepper, and purée them. Keep warm. Wash and drain 12 large basil leaves. Cut the bacon slices in half. Shell the scampi and wrap each piece of tail meat in a basil leaf and half a bacon slice. Secure with a toothpick. Sauté the scampi in an ungreased nonstick frying pan over high heat for 3 minutes on each side. Shape a piece of aluminum foil into a ring about 1 inch (3 centimeters) high and use this as a mold to make two round patties of puréed potato. Put each one on a serving plate, and pile the sautéed scampi on top. Moisten with the olive oil, sprinkle with the kosher salt and crushed mixed peppercorns, and serve immediately.

Cook fresh live scampi for 2 minutes in boiling salted water, drain, cool to lukewarm, and shell.

Scallops with ginger and lime

Peel the lime with a sharp knife or vegetable parer, cut the zest into fine strips, and blanch for 1 minute in boiling water. Drain. Squeeze and reserve the lime juice. Peel and grate the ginger root. Wipe the scallops, place in a bowl with the lime juice, zest, grated ginger, chili powder, salt and pepper, and put in the refrigerator to chill. Meanwhile, peel and slice the celeriac and cook in a pot of boiling salted water for 15 minutes. Drain and purée in the blender with 2 tablespoons olive oil, salt and pepper. Remove the scallops from the marinade and pat dry on kitchen paper. Sauté for 1 minute on each side in 1 tablespoon olive oil, remove from the pot and keep warm. Deglaze the sauté pan with the scallop marinade, scraping well with a wooden spoon. Gradually stir in the butter to make a smooth sauce. Arrange the celery purée on serving plates, garnish with the scallops, and coat with the sauce.

Ingredients

- *1 lime*
- *1 small piece fresh ginger root*
- *8 scallops, shelled*
- *1 pinch chili powder*
- *salt, pepper*
- *1 quarter of a celeriac*
- *3 tablespoons olive oil*
- *3 tablespoons (45 g) butter*

49

The scallop season varies from country to country. Out of season, it is possible to use frozen scallops, although they are not such good quality.

John Dory fillets with orange butter

Ingredients

- *1 orange*
- *½ bunch chervil*
- *1 John Dory weighing about 1½ lb. (600–700 g), cleaned and gutted*
- *1 tablespoon olive oil*
- *salt, pepper*
- *¼ cup (5 cl) light cream*
- *a few saffron threads*
- *1 teaspoon green peppercorns, milled*
- *3 tablespoons unsalted butter*

Preheat oven to 400°F (200°C).

Peel the orange with a vegetable parer or sharp knife, cut the zest into fine strips, and blanch for 1 minute in boiling salted water. Cut the orange in two, slice one half and squeeze the juice of the other half. Wash, drain, and chop the chervil. Lay the John Dory on a sheet of aluminum foil, place the orange slices and half of the chopped chervil inside the fish, brush with the olive oil, season with salt and pepper. Cover the John Dory with a second sheet of aluminum foil and pinch the edges closed to make an airtight package. Place in a shallow ovenproof pan and bake for about 20 minutes. Meanwhile, prepare the sauce. Combine the orange juice, orange rind, cream, saffron, and milled green peppercorns in a small pot. Season with salt. Reduce this mixture over a medium heat for 5 minutes, stirring constantly with a wire whisk. Gradually whisk in the butter. When the fish is done, remove from oven and unwrap. Carefully remove the skin and detach the fillets. Arrange the fillets on two serving plates, garnish with the orange slices, sprinkle with the rest of the chervil, and coat with the sauce.

Tender shredded Savoy cabbage sautéed in butter is a good accompaniment to this dish.

Quail in Baume de Venise stuffed with arugula, apples, and currants

Ingredients

- *1 teaspoon currants*
- *1 tablespoon Baume de Venise dessert wine*
- *2 dessert apples*
- *juice of ½ lemon*
- *1 teaspoon pine nuts*
- *1 bunch arugula, washed and drained*
- *2 oven-ready quails*
- *salt, pepper*
- *2 thin slices smoked bacon*
- *2 tablespoons butter*
- *1 tablespoon olive oil*
- *¼ chicken bouillon cube*

Soak the currants in the Baume de Venise. Peel and slice the apples; moisten with the lemon juice. Brown the pine nuts in a frying pan for a few minutes. Tear the arugula into small pieces. Stuff the quails with the arugula, currants, and pine nuts. Season with salt and pepper. Wrap a slice of bacon around each quail and truss with culinary string. Melt the butter and olive oil in a cast-iron casserole over medium heat. Brown the quails all over in the hot fat, reduce the heat, add the apples, and cover. When the apples are lightly browned, dissolve the bouillon cube in ¼ cup of boiling water and add to the casserole. Simmer for 20 minutes, checking frequently. When ready, arrange the quails on serving plates and garnish with the apples.

A fragrant Muscat wine of the Frontignan type may be substituted for the Baume de Venise.

Pears stuffed with blue-cheese mousse

Ingredients

- *2 juicy pears*
- *juice of ½ lemon*
- *½ cup (10 cl) heavy cream*
- *¼ lb. (100 g) Lacceuil blue cheese*
- *chopped chives for garnish*

Chill a mixing bowl in the refrigerator. Peel the pears, leaving them whole, then cut off a slice just below the top and put on one side. Hollow out the centers, removing all the seeds. Moisten with the lemon juice. Place the cream and blue cheese in the chilled bowl and beat with an electric beater until light and firm. Chill. Just before serving, fill the pears with the blue-cheese mousse, replace the tops, and garnish with the chives.

Bartlett pears are ideal for this recipe.

Lamb sweetbreads
with a salad of fava beans

Ingredients

- *¾ lb. (300 g) lamb sweetbreads, trimmed by the butcher*
- *1 lb. (450 g) shelled fava beans*
- *2 tablespoons olive oil*
- *1 tablespoon balsamic vinegar*
- *½ bunch chervil*
- *½ teaspoon kosher salt*
- *½ teaspoon crushed mixed peppercorns*

Wash and drain the sweetbreads, drop into a pot of boiling salted water and poach for 1 minute. Remove from the pot and drain. Cook the shelled beans in a pot of boiling salted water for 15–20 minutes. When cooked, drain and remove the tough outer coat from each bean, which should be firm and very green. Coat the beans with 1 tablespoon olive oil and keep warm. Cut the lamb sweetbreads across into slices and sauté in a frying pan with 1 tablespoon olive oil, turning them often, until golden and crusted. Remove the sweetbreads from the frying pan and drain on paper towel. Deglaze the pan with the balsamic vinegar and 1 tablespoon water. Pour the pan juices over the beans. Pile the beans onto serving plates and place the sweetbreads on top. Sprinkle with the chervil, kosher salt, and crushed mixed peppercorns. Serve immediately.

You can use frozen fava beans for this dish when fresh ones are not in season.

56

Summer-fruit cocktail in Sauterne jelly

Ingredients

- *½ lb. (225 g) tart apples*
- *1½ cups (35 cl) Sauterne or Montbazillac wine*
- *1 cup (250 g) coarse granulated sugar*
- *1 clove*
- *½ cinnamon stick*
- *4 oz. (100 g) wild strawberries*
- *2 oz. (60 g) raspberries*
- *4 oz. (100 g) red currants*

Peel, core, and dice the apples, place in a small pot with the wine, bring to a boil, reduce the heat, cover, and simmer for 20 minutes. Press the contents of the pot through a very fine sieve to extract the juice. Stir the sugar into the juice, and add the clove and cinnamon stick. Bring to a boil and then simmer for 5 minutes. Cool, skim, and remove the clove and cinnamon stick. Pour into a bowl and set aside until it begins to form a jelly. Wash and wipe the berries. Pour the jelly into parfait glasses and garnish with the berries. Serve chilled, accompanied with small sweet dessert cookies.

Pour any leftover wine-apple jelly into a jar, seal it tightly, and use later to spread on toast.

Champagne and tangerine cream

Ingredients

- *½ organic lemon*
- *½ bottle chilled Champagne*
- *¼ cup (5 cl) tangerine-cream liqueur*

Cut the zest from the half lemon with a vegetable parer or sharp knife. Pour the tangerine-cream liqueur into two glasses. Add the Champagne and twists of lemon zest. Serve immediately.

For a particularly refreshing drink, substitute tangerine juice for the tangerine liqueur.

58

Chocolate heart with raspberries

Preheat oven to 300°F (150°C).

Separate the egg yolks from the whites. Melt the chocolate in the top of a double boiler. Remove from heat and whisk in the egg yolks, butter, sugar, raspberry liqueur, and flour. Whisk the egg whites until stiff and fold into the chocolate mixture. Butter a heart-shaped or round cake tin. Pour the mixture into the tin and bake for 40 minutes. Check that it is ready by inserting the tip of a sharp knife. The cake should be slightly runny in the center. If using a round cake tin, cut a piece of cardboard into a heart-shaped pattern approximately the same size as the cake. Remove the cake from the tin, place the cardboard pattern on top of it, and use a sharp knife to cut out a heart. Cool. Wash and drain the raspberries. Just before serving, arrange the raspberries evenly over the top of the cake. Dredge with confectioners' sugar and serve immediately.

Ingredients

- *3 eggs*
- *4 oz. (100 g) bitter chocolate*
- *4 oz. (100 g) unsalted butter*
- *½ cup (100 g) granulated sugar*
- *1 teaspoon raspberry liqueur*
- *1 tablespoon flour*
- *5 oz. (150 g) fresh raspberries*
- *1 teaspoon confectioners' (icing) sugar*

A few fresh raspberries can be added to the chocolate mixture before baking.

In the Kitchen

For an informal dinner at the kitchen table,
serve light wines such as Chinon, Sauvignon,
Beaujolais Village, or Côtes de Provence.

French toast with sautéed bacon

62

Ingredients

- *4 slices plain white bread*
- *3 eggs*
- *½ cup (10 cl) milk*
- *2 pinches salt*
- *8 thin slices smoked bacon*
- *½ teaspoon chili powder*
- *chopped chives*

Use a serrated knife to cut the slices of bread in half and remove the crusts. In a shallow soup plate, beat together the eggs, milk, and salt. Place a nonstick frying pan over medium heat. Dip the slices of bread in the milk-and-egg mixture and cook in the hot pan until golden, turning several times. Meanwhile, sauté the bacon in an ungreased frying pan and drain on paper towel. Garnish the French toast with the sautéed bacon, sprinkle with the chili powder and chopped chives. Serve immediately, for breakfast.

You can make a more elegant version of this recipe by substituting brioche for the plain white bread.

Eggplant papillote with goat cheese, thyme, and olives

Ingredients

- *1 eggplant*
- *2 small creamy goat cheeses*
- *3 tablespoons olive oil*
- *2 sprigs thyme*
- *8 black olives*
- *salt, pepper*

Preheat broiler.

Cut the eggplant lengthwise into 4 thin slices. Using a pastry brush, brush both sides with olive oil. Place on a baking sheet covered with ovenproof paper and grill under the broiler, turning once, until both sides are golden.

Preheat the oven to 350°F (180°C).

Lay two eggplant slices crosswise on top of each other and put one of the goat cheeses in the center. Sprinkle with thyme leaves and season with salt and pepper. Fold the four arms of the cross around the cheese to make a parcel, and tie with culinary string. Do the same with the other eggplant slices and the second cheese. Place the papillotes in an ovenproof dish, drizzle with olive oil, and surround with the olives. Bake for 10 minutes. Serve accompanied by a salad.

Be sure to choose a well-shaped, firm, and shiny eggplant for this dish.

64

Beef carpaccio with Parmesan cheese, olives, sun-dried tomatoes, and basil

Ingredients

- *2 oz. (60 g) sun-dried tomatoes*
- *2 oz. (60 g) Parmesan cheese*
- *8 black olives, pitted*
- *½ lb. (225 g) beef carpaccio*
- *several basil leaves*
- *½ teaspoon crushed mixed peppercorns*
- *½ teaspoon kosher salt*
- *2 tablespoons olive oil*

Using a pair of scissors, cut the sun-dried tomatoes into thin strips. Cut slivers of Parmesan cheese with a vegetable parer. Chop the olives. Arrange slices of the beef carpaccio on each plate. Garnish with the sun-dried tomatoes, slivers of Parmesan cheese, chopped olives, basil leaves, and a sprinkling of kosher salt and crushed mixed peppercorns. Drizzle the olive oil over all and serve immediately.

If you cannot get hold of pre-sliced carpaccio, buy a small piece of beef fillet and freeze until it is hard enough to cut into very thin slices.

Chicken skewers in a hot marinade
with red pepper, scallion, and ginger

66

Ingredients

- *2 chicken breasts*
- *1 small red pepper*
- *1 teaspoon curry powder*
- *1 teaspoon turmeric*
- *1 teaspoon paprika*
- *2 sprigs of thyme*
- *1 scallion*
- *1½ inch (4 cm) length of ginger root*
- *juice of ½ lime*
- *2 tablespoons olive oil*
- *1 teaspoon soy sauce*
- *salt, pepper*
- *skewers*

Cut the red pepper in half, remove the seeds and tough core, and slice. Cut the chicken breasts into large chunks. Place the chunks of chicken and slices of pepper in a dish, sprinkle with the curry powder, turmeric, and paprika. Wash, drain and strip off the leaves from the thyme sprigs, peel and chop the scallion, peel the ginger and cut into small strips. Add all these to the bowl, together with the lime juice, olive oil, soy sauce, salt and pepper. Mix all together well, cover with plastic wrap, and chill for 1 hour. Remove the chunks of chicken from the marinade and thread onto skewers. Preheat the broiler. Place the skewers in a shallow ovenproof pan and grill for 10 minutes under the broiler, turning frequently. Serve immediately.

Use disposable wooden skewers, which are more hygienic than metal ones and do not conduct the heat. For a decorative touch, alternate the chunks of chicken with slices of lime.

Spinach salad with egg, smoked duck breast, and Roquefort

Wash and drain the spinach leaves. Remove and discard the fat from the duck breast, separate the slices. Crumble the Roquefort cheese. Prepare a vinaigrette dressing with the peanut oil, wine vinegar, salt and pepper. Immerse the eggs in a pot of boiling water, remove from heat, and allow to stand for 6–8 minutes. Arrange mounds of spinach leaves on two serving plates, top with the sliced duck breast and crumbled pieces of Roquefort. Shell the eggs (this is easier if you plunge them into cold water first), cut them in half and place on top of the other ingredients. Sprinkle with the crushed peanuts and chives, and dress with the vinaigrette. Serve immediately.

Ingredients

- *½ lb. (225 g) young spinach leaves*
- *½ smoked duck breast, sliced*
- *4 oz. (100 g) Roquefort cheese*
- *3 tablespoons peanut oil*
- *1 tablespoon wine vinegar*
- *salt, pepper*
- *2 eggs*
- *1 tablespoon peanuts, shelled, blanched, and crushed*
- *chopped chives*

Instead of Roquefort you can use other types of blue cheese such as Auvergne, Bresse, Stilton, etc.

Fresh tuna pizzas

70

Ingredients

- *½ lb. fillet of fresh red tuna*
- *2 tablespoons olive oil*
- *1 Bermuda (red) onion*
- *2 pinches granulated sugar*
- *1 pinch chili powder*
- *salt, pepper*
- *7 oz. (200 g) ready-to-cook dough*
- *2 teaspoons tapenade*
  (black olive paste)

Preheat oven to 400°F (200°C).

Wipe the fillet of tuna, cover in plastic wrap, and place in the freezer for 30 minutes. Peel and chop the onion. Place 1 tablespoon olive oil in a pot with the chopped onion, sugar, chili powder, salt and pepper. Stir all the ingredients together well, cover, and simmer for 20 minutes. To make the pizza bases, divide the dough into two equal parts and roll into identically sized circles. Place on a baking sheet lined with ovenproof paper and spread each one with a layer of the cooked onions and then a layer of tapenade. Bake for 10–12 minutes. Remove the tuna from the freezer and cut into very thin slices. When the pizzas are ready, take out of the oven, garnish with the slices of tuna arranged like the spokes of a wheel, and return to the oven for 1 minute. Drizzle with the remaining olive oil and serve immediately.

When buying fresh tuna, ask for a fillet cut from the center of the fish (the meatiest and most tender part).

Tagliatellini with sage and pancetta

Ingredients

- *½ bunch fresh sage*
- *4 slices pancetta ham*
- *3 tablespoons olive oil*
- *7 oz. (200 g) fresh tagliatellini pasta*
- *2 tablespoons ricotta cheese*
- *2 tablespoons butter*
- *2 oz. (60 g) grated Parmesan cheese*
- *salt, pepper*

Wash and drain the sage leaves. Sauté the slices of pancetta on both sides in an ungreased frying pan. Drain on paper towel. Heat 2 tablespoons olive oil in the frying pan, add the sage leaves, and sauté for 1 minute. Drain on paper towel. Cook the pasta according to the instructions on the pack in a large pot of boiling salted water to which 1 tablespoon of olive oil has been added. When cooked, drain, and add the ricotta and butter. Stir together well. Heap the pasta on two serving plates and top each pile with the pancetta, sage leaves, grated Parmesan, salt and pepper. Serve immediately.

You can substitute mascarpone (or olive oil) for the ricotta.

Compote of tomatoes
with mozzarella, tapenade, and basil

Wash the tomatoes, cut out the stem end, and cut in half horizontally, then place in a pan with 2 tablespoons olive oil and simmer for 10 minutes until soft. Remove from pan and allow to cool. Place the bottom halves of the tomatoes on serving plates, lay a slice of mozzarella on top, and finish with the upper half of the tomatoes. Use toothpicks to hold the layers together. Surround the tomatoes with the tapenade and moisten with 2 tablespoons olive oil. Garnish with the basil leaves, and sprinkle with salt and pepper. Serve with 2 slices of toast.

Ingredients

- *4 medium-sized vine tomatoes*
- *4 tablespoons olive oil*
- *4 square slices buffalo mozzarella*
- *2 tablespoons tapenade*
  (black olive paste)
- *several basil leaves*
- *salt, pepper*

Buffalo mozzarella is slightly more expensive than cows' milk mozzarella, but the quality is vastly superior.

Baked red mullet, shallot butter with saffron, and fennel compote

Ingredients

- *1 large fennel bulb*
- *1 tablespoon olive oil*
- *5 tablespoons (75 g) butter*
- *2 red mullets, cleaned and scaled*
- *1 small shallot*
- *1 sachet powdered saffron*
- *1 pinch chili pepper*
- *salt, pepper*

Preheat oven to 400°F (200°C).

Trim the fennel, setting aside the leafy stems. Chop the bulb. Place the olive oil and 2 tablespoons of the butter in a small pan, add the chopped fennel, season with salt and pepper. Bring to a simmer over a low heat, cover, and cook for 10 minutes, stirring occasionally. Keep warm. Rub the red mullets with olive oil and place on a sheet of aluminum foil. Insert a fennel stem inside each fish. Fold and pinch the foil to make an airtight package. Bake for 15 minutes. Peel and chop the shallot. Mash the remaining butter with a fork, add the chopped shallot, saffron, and chili pepper. Season with salt and pepper. When the mullets are done, remove from the aluminum foil and place on serving plates. Garnish with a dab of the saffron butter and the fennel compote.

When you purchase red mullet, ask that the livers be included. When the livers are placed inside the fish before baking, they add an additional touch of delicious flavor.

White-wine cocktail with Perrier and lemon

Ingredients

- *½ lemon*
- *8 fl. oz. (25 cl) Perrier water*
- *8 fl. oz. (25 cl) dry white wine*
- *several mint leaves*

Wash the lemon, wipe dry, and slice. Pour the chilled white wine into two wine glasses, add the chilled Perrier water and lemon slices. Garnish with the mint leaves and serve immediately.

Choose organic lemons. For nonorganic lemons, wash them with unscented soap in hot water and rinse well before using.

Finger toasts with sardine butter, radishes, and pink peppercorns

Ingredients

- *4 sardines in oil*
- *juice of ½ organic lemon*
- *2 tablespoons butter*
- *1 teaspoon pink peppercorns*
- *salt, pepper*
- *2 large slices country bread*
- *12 red radishes*

Drain the sardines, add the lemon juice, and mash with a fork. Cream the butter and add to the sardines, again mashing with a fork. Crush the peppercorns, add to the sardine butter, and season with salt and pepper. Chill. Just before serving, toast the slices of bread and slice the radishes. Spread the toast with the sardine butter and garnish with the radish slices. Cut the toast into 3 or 4 finger slices and serve.

If you like hot, spicy flavors, try adding a dash of Tabasco to the sardine butter.

Egg custard with lemon

80

Ingredients

- *2 cups (½ l) milk*
- *3 eggs*
- *1 vanilla bean (pod)*
- *1 teaspoon lemon juice*
- *zest of 1 lemon*
- *5 tablespoons granulated sugar*

Preheat the oven to 300°F (150°C).

Pour the milk into a pot. Split the vanilla bean in two lengthwise, scrape the seeds into the milk, add the bean, and heat without allowing to boil. Cut the lemon zest into fine strips, blanch for 1 minute in boiling water, and drain. Beat the eggs and sugar together in a bowl. Whisk in the warm milk, and add the lemon juice and zest. Pour this mixture into two individual ramekins, place the ramekins in a pan of boiling water (the water should come half way up the sides of the ramekins), and bake in the oven for 25 minutes. Remove from the oven and cool before serving.

For a poor man's version of crème brûlée, sprinkle the cooled custard with brown sugar and place under the broiler for 1–2 minutes, checking constantly, until the surface is bubbling and golden.

Tiny coconut hearts

Preheat oven to 400°F (200°C).

Cream the eggs and sugar. Add the flour, yeast, grated coconut, and 3 tablespoons melted butter. Blend until smooth. Grease heart-shaped molds with the remaining butter, fill with the cake mixture, and bake for approximately 20 minutes. Test with a knife to see if the cakes are done. Remove the cakes from the molds and allow to cool. Garnish with a few slices of kumquat (optional). These little cakes can be accompanied with custard sauce (see recipe on page 30).

Ingredients

- *2 eggs*
- *6 tablespoons granulated sugar*
- *½ cup (110 g) flour*
- *½ packet (5 g) yeast*
- *3 tablespoons grated coconut*
- *4 tablespoons butter*
- *1 kumquat (optional)*

This is the cake mixture used to make Madeleine cakes,
with the addition of the grated coconut.

A Riverside Lunch

It's summer, a time for enjoying refreshing
wines—rosé, red, or white—such as Bandol,
Alsatian Muscat, Chablis, or Côtes du Rhône Village.

Surprise tomatoes
with goat cheese and herbs

86

Ingredients

- *4 vine tomatoes*
- *2 sprigs basil*
- *2 sprigs flat parsley*
- *a few chives*
- *2 sprigs tarragon*
- *2 sprigs chervil*
- *1 teaspoon crushed mixed peppercorns*
- *½ teaspoon kosher salt*
- *7 oz. (200 g) fresh goat cheese*
- *4 tablespoons olive oil*

Immerse the tomatoes for 1 minute in boiling water. Drain and peel, leaving the stem in place. Wash and drain the herbs, set half on one side, and chop the remainder. Mash the goat cheese with a fork, add the chopped herbs, crushed mixed peppercorns, and 2 tablespoons olive oil, and mix together thoroughly. Cut a small slice off the base of each tomato and use a teaspoon to scoop out the center. Fill the tomatoes with the goat cheese mixture and arrange on serving plates with the stem uppermost. Drizzle with olive oil and garnish with the rest of the herbs. The tomatoes will look as if they are whole and intact, and the goat cheese stuffing will come as a surprise!

Choose tomatoes that are ripe but firm, bright red, and fragrant.

Prawn toasts with avocado

Ingredients

- *1 avocado*
- *½ bunch fresh coriander*
- *juice of ½ lemon*
- *3 drops Tabasco*
- *12 cooked prawns*
- *3 slices country bread*
- *½ teaspoon crushed mixed peppercorns*
- *½ teaspoon kosher salt*

Peel and pit the avocado. Wash, drain, and chop the fresh coriander. Mash the avocado, moisten with the lemon juice, add the chopped coriander and Tabasco. Peel the prawns and set the tail meat aside. Toast the bread. Spread each slice with a layer of avocado purée, garnish with the prawn tails, and sprinkle with crushed mixed peppercorns and kosher salt. Serve immediately.

Make these at the last moment so they do not have time to become soggy.

Green-and-red pasta salad with Tabasco

Ingredients

- *½ bunch red radishes*
- *6 chives*
- *1 slice boiled ham about ¼-inch (½ cm) thick*
- *2 small cucumbers*
- *1 egg yolk*
- *1 teaspoon mustard*
- *pepper*
- *4 tablespoons sunflower oil*
- *a few drops vinegar*
- *7 oz. (200 g) fresh pasta*
- *½ container plain yogurt*
- *4 drops Tabasco*

Wash, drain, trim, and slice the radishes. Wash, drain, and chop the chives. Dice the ham. Wash, wipe, and slice the cucumbers. Prepare a mayonnaise with the egg yolk, mustard, and pepper; gradually add the sunflower oil, ending with a few drops of vinegar. Cook the pasta according to the instructions on the pack in a large pan of boiling salted water, drain in a colander, and rinse under cold water. In a serving dish, combine the mayonnaise with the yogurt and Tabasco. Add the pasta and stir. Garnish with the radishes, chives, ham, and cucumber slices. Serve immediately or chill until serving time.

Pasta shapes such as macaroni or small shells are most suitable for this dish as they will hold the mayonnaise well.

Tuna *tartare*

Prepare a mayonnaise-type sauce with the egg yolk, mustard, wasabi, salt and pepper. Gradually add the sunflower oil, whisking all the time. Add the lemon juice and Tabasco. Chill. Dice the tuna. Chop the seaweed finely. Mix the tuna and the seaweed into the sauce. Chill thoroughly. Serve with two large slices of toast.

Ingredients

- *1 egg yolk*
- *1 teaspoon mustard*
- *½ teaspoon wasabi*
  (Japanese green mustard) -
- *salt, pepper*
- *sunflower oil*
- *juice of ½ lemon*
- *3 drops Tabasco*
- *7 oz. (200 g) raw tuna*
- *3 oz. (60 g) seaweed*

91

Seaweed such as salcornia (also known as glasswort or march samphire) or rock samphire are recommended for this recipe. They can be found pickled in the gourmet-food sections of some supermarkets if you cannot find them fresh. Well-drained capers may be substituted for the seaweed.

Salmon crêpes with herbs

92

Ingredients

- *½ cup (125 g) flour*
- *1 cup (25 cl) milk*
- *2 eggs*
- *1 tablespoon melted butter*
- *½ tablespoon herb-flavored Bison vodka*
- *¼ teaspoon salt*
- *2 sprigs chervil*
- *2 sprigs flat parsley*
- *a few chives*
- *2 sprigs tarragon*
- *2 sprigs dill*
- *2 tablespoons olive oil*
- *2 slices marinated or smoked salmon*
- *½ lemon*

Prepare the batter for the crêpes by combining the flour and milk in a bowl. Add the eggs, melted butter, vodka, and salt. Whisk until smooth. Let sit for 1 hour. Wash and drain the herbs, take off the leaves from the stems and spread them on a piece of paper towel. Oil a nonstick frying pan and place over medium heat. Pour a little of the batter into the pan, and sprinkle on a few herbs. When the crêpe hardens and begins to color around the edges, carefully turn it over and cook the second side until done. Slide the crêpe from the pan onto a plate. Repeat until all the batter has been used up. Roll up the crêpes and arrange on two serving plates with the smoked or marinated salmon. Garnish with lemon wedges and sprinkle with the remaining herbs.

Grease the crêpe pan by dipping a clean cloth or piece of paper towel into some olive oil in a small bowl and rubbing it all over the surface.

94

Piquillo peppers stuffed
with cod and mozzarella

Ingredients

- 1 fish bouillon cube
- 5 oz. (150 g) cod fillet
- 2 sprigs basil
- 6 canned piquillo peppers
- 2 mozzarella cheeses
- ½ teaspoon kosher salt
- ½ teaspoon crushed mixed peppercorns
- 2 tablespoons olive oil
- ¾ cup (20 cl) heavy cream
- ½ teaspoon granulated sugar

Preheat oven to 400°F (200°C).

Dissolve the bouillon cube in a pot of boiling water. Place the cod fillet in the liquid, bring back to a boil, reduce the heat, and allow to simmer for 5 minutes more. Drain and set aside. Wash, drain, and chop the basil. Drain the piquillo peppers. Mash the mozzarella with a fork. Flake the cod and add to the mozzarella with the chopped basil, kosher salt, and crushed mixed peppercorns. Rub an ovenproof dish with olive oil. Carefully fill 4 of the piquillo peppers with the cod stuffing and arrange in the oiled dish. Bake for 10 minutes. Meanwhile, purée the 2 remaining piquillos in a blender with the cream and sugar. Transfer to a pan and heat gently. Place 2 baked piquillos on each serving plate and serve with the lukewarm purée.

Canned piquillo peppers from Spain are available at specialty grocery stores.

Barbecued marinated fillet of duck with snow pcas

Wash and wipc thc lime, lemon, and grapefruit, peel with a vegetable parer and dice the zest finely. Squeeze the juice from all the fruits. Peel and dice the ginger root. Put the duck fillets in a shallow dish and add the zest, fruit juice, ginger, honey, soy sauce, and olive oil. Place in the refrigerator and marinate for at least 1 hour, turning the fillets occasionally. Wash and trim the snow peas, cook for 6 minutes in a pot of boiling salted water. Keep warm. Meanwhile, light the barbecue. Drain the duck fillets on a grooved wooden board to catch all the marinade. Pour into a small pan and add the marinade remaining in the dish; reduce over a high heat for 5 minutes to make a sauce. Grill the duck fillets on the barbecue for 5 minutes each side. Serve immediately with the snow peas and sauce.

Ingredients

97

- ½ lime
- ½ lemon
- ½ pink grapefruit
- 1 piece ginger root about
  1 inch (3 cm) long
- 10 oz. (300 g) duck fillets
- 2 tablespoons honey
- 1 tablespoon soy sauce
- 2 tablespoons olive oil
- 10 oz. (300 g) snow peas

If you do not have a barbecue, you can place the duck fillets on a baking sheet covered with aluminum foil and grill under the broiler.

98

Salad of grapes, goat cheese, and pancetta

Ingredients

- *2 oz. (60 g) mixed lettuce leaves*
- *12 large grapes*
- *(Italia or similar variety)*
- *1 small dry goat cheese*
- *6 slices pancetta*
- *1 garlic clove*
- *3 tablespoons olive oil*
- *1 level teaspoon Dijon mustard*
- *1 level tablespoon balsamic vinegar*
- *salt, pepper*

Wash and drain the lettuce. Peel the grapes. Cut the goat cheese into thin slivers—this is best done with a vegetable parer. Fry the pancetta slices on both sides in a nonstick frying pan, drain on paper towel. Peel the garlic clove and leave whole. Prepare a vinaigrette with the olive oil, mustard, vinegar, garlic, salt and pepper. Heap the lettuce on two serving plates and garnish with the pancetta, grapes, and slivers of goat cheese. Remove the garlic clove from the vinaigrette and pour the dressing over the salad. Serve immediately.

If a milder vinaigrette is preferred, add 1 tablespoon water.

Cocktail of melon juice, vodka, and cassis

Ingredients

- *1 very ripe Cavaillon melon*
- *½ cup (10 cl) unflavored vodka*
- *¼ cup (6 cl) cassis (blackcurrant liqueur) or blackcurrant purée*
- *2 sprigs mint (optional)*
- *ice cubes*

Peel the melon, scoop out the seeds, dice the flesh, and purée in a blender. Pour the vodka into 2 glasses. Add the melon purée and cassis or blackcurrant purée. Place a few ice cubes in each glass, and garnish with the mint leaves. Serve immediately.

Melon stems fall off naturally as the fruit ripens, so look for one without a stem—this is a sure sign that the fruit is very ripe.

Motoko's tiny pastry hearts

Preheat oven to 350°F (180°C).

Beat 2 tablespoons of water into the egg yolk. Crush the crystallized violets and mix with the sugar crystals. Roll out the pastry and place on a baking sheet. Using a heart-shaped cookie cutter, cut out tiny pastry hearts. Carefully remove the pastry trimmings around each one. Glaze the hearts with the egg-and-water mix, then sprinkle with the sugar crystals. Bake for 10–15 minutes. Remove the hearts from the baking sheet and allow to cool. Serve with ice cream or custard.

Ingredients

- *1 egg yolk*
- *1½ tablespoons crystallized violets*
- *2 tablespoons (30 g) colored sugar crystals*
- *1 sheet ready-to-use puff pastry*

You can make your own all-color sugar crystals by crushing sour balls with crystallized mimosa or violets.

Peaches in blackcurrant sauce

Ingredients

- *7 oz. (200 g) blackcurrants*
- *2 yellow or white peaches*
- *⅓ cup (100 g) granulated sugar*
- *several mint leaves*

Wash and drain the blackcurrants, purée in a blender, and transfer the contents to a small pot. Bring to a boil, reduce the heat, and simmer for 10 minutes. Remove from the heat and pass through a fine sieve over a bowl to extract all the seeds. Allow the purée to cool. Immerse the peaches for 2 minutes in boiling water, remove, and peel. Make a syrup by boiling the sugar with ⅓ cup water. Reduce to a simmer and cook the peaches in the syrup until they are soft but still hold their shape. Drain the peaches, place on dessert plates, and surround with the blackcurrant purée. Garnish with the mint leaves. Serve chilled.

The blackcurrant purée can be prepared in advance. After being cooked for 10 minutes, it will keep for several days in the refrigerator.

Lemon granitas with verbena

Ingredients

- *1 sprig verbena*
- *⅓ cup (90 g) granulated sugar*
- *1 cup (25 cl) spring water*
- *2 organic lemons*

Wash and drain the verbena, and remove the leaves. Place the water and sugar in a small pot, bring to a boil, lower the heat, and simmer until reduced by one-fourth. Add the verbena leaves to the syrup, cool, and strain. Squeeze the lemons and stir the juice into the cooled syrup. Pour this mixture into an ice-cube tray and chill in the freezer for 2 hours. As the mixture freezes, break it up from time to time with a fork. Scoop into parfait glasses and serve immediately.

Place the parfait glasses in the freezer for a few minutes
just before serving. Granitas should be served well chilled.

Orange-and-lemon cakes

Ingredients

- *3 tablespoons candied lemon peel*
- *3 tablespoons candied orange peel*
- *4 tablespoons unsalted butter*
- *2 egg whites*
- *5 tablespoons granulated sugar*
- *pinch salt*
- *1 oz. (25 g) ground almonds*
- *2 tablespoons flour*
- *1 teaspoon baking powder*

Preheat oven to 400°F (200°C).

Slice the candied orange and lemon peel finely. Melt the butter in a small pot. In a bowl, whisk the egg whites with the sugar and salt until stiff. Fold in the candied peel, melted butter, ground almonds flour and baking powder. Grease several small flat muffin tins, fill with the cake mixture, and bake for 15 minutes or until the tip of a sharp knife inserted into the center of a cake comes out clean. Serve the cakes warm, or cool and store in an airtight tin.

To make your own candied peel, cut the zest of citrus fruits into fine strips
and simmer in a syrup made with water and sugar for 15 minutes.

Bedside Dinners

Special moments call for special wines—Sancerre,
Alsace Riesling, or Champagne for the whites,
Merlot or Burgundy for the reds.

Tiny fish-roe treats

Ingredients

- 1 small cucumber
- ¾ cup (20 cl) crème fraîche
- 4 teaspoons trout roe
- 4 teaspoons herring roe
- 4 teaspoons salmon roe
- a few chives
- 2 slices white bread
- 8 rose petals
- 4 tiny blintzes

Wash and wipe the cucumber, and cut into thin slices. Wash, drain, and chop the chives. Place three cucumber slices on top of each other in a spiral shape, spread with crème fraîche, garnish with a spoonful of trout roe, and sprinkle with chives. Do this until all the cucumber slices are used up, arrange on a serving plate, and chill until serving time.

Preheat oven to 400°F (200°C).

Wrap the blintzes in aluminum foil and heat in the oven for 10 minutes. Remove and cool until lukewarm. Meanwhile, toast the slices of bread, cut off the crusts, and cut each slice into two equal halves. Place a rose petal on each piece, top with crème fraîche, garnish with a teaspoon of herring roe, and set aside. When the blintzes are cool enough, spread each one with ½ teaspoon crème fraîche, and garnish with a teaspoon of salmon roe. Add to the other prepared treats and serve immediately.

The blintzes can be cut into heart shapes with a cookie cutter.

Smoked-salmon *temaki* with avocado and dill cream

Ingredients

- *1 avocado*
- *juice of ½ lemon*
- *2 sprigs dill*
- *2 slices smoked salmon*
- *½ cup (10 cl) crème fraîche*
- *½ teaspoon crushed mixed peppercorns*

Cut the avocado in half, remove the pit, slice the flesh into lengthwise strips and sprinkle with the lemon juice. Wash and drain the dill, removing the stems. Divide each slice of salmon into 2 rectangles. Arrange each rectangle on a sheet of plastic film wrap, spread the center with crème fraîche, garnish with the avocado strips and dill, and sprinkle with the crushed mixed peppercorns. Roll the salmon into a cigar shape and wrap tightly in the plastic wrap, twisting the ends closed. Chill. At serving time, remove the plastic wrap and use a serrated knife to cut the salmon rolls into *temaki* slices. Serve immediately.

Japanese *temaki* are usually made with seaweed. Asian grocery stores and the gourmet-food sections of some supermarkets sell small flexible bamboo mats for rolling up temaki, which produce better-shaped rolls.

Champagne cocktail with raspberries

Ingredients

- *6 fresh raspberries*
- *½ bottle chilled dry (brut) Champagne*

Wash the raspberries and drain them on paper towel. Pour the Champagne into flutes, add the raspberries, and serve at once.

For additional flavor, splash a little raspberry liqueur into the bottom of the flutes before adding the Champagne.

Serves **2**   Preparation time: **15 minutes**   Cooking time: **5 minutes**

112

Prawns with green chili pepper paste

Peel the prawns, discard the heads, and leave the tips of the tails intact. Sprinkle the tail meat with a little lime juice. Wash and drain the mint, and remove the leaves. Trim and slice the chili, discarding the seeds and membrane. Blend the mint, chili, and remaining lime juice to a fairly thick paste. Heat the olive oil in a frying pan and sauté the prawns for 5 minutes, turning once. Drain on paper towel. If you are using uncooked prawn wafers, fry them according to the instructions on the pack. Spread each wafer with the chili paste and garnish with a sautéed prawn.

Ingredients

- *12 large cooked prawns*
- *juice of 2 limes*
- *½ bunch fresh mint*
- *1 small green chili*
- *2 tablespoons olive oil*
- *12 prawn wafers*

It is a good idea to wear kitchen gloves when preparing chilis as the juice can be highly irritating to the eyes. Some people believe that the irritating components in the juice are eliminated if you run your fingers through your hair!

Chicken soup with ginger and shitake mushrooms

Peel and chop the ginger root. Rinse the mushrooms, wipe dry, chop, and sauté in a frying pan with the butter for a few minutes. Set aside. Slice the chicken breasts. In a pot, dissolve the bouillon cube in 3 cups (75 cl) of boiling water, add the chopped ginger and chicken, and simmer for about 10 minutes. Add the mushrooms and simmer for 5 minutes more. Pour into soup plates and garnish with fresh coriander leaves. Serve immediately.

Ingredients

- *1 piece of ginger root, about ¾ inch (2 cm) long*
- *4 oz. (100 g) Japanese shitake mushrooms*
- *1 tablespoon butter*
- *2 chicken breasts*
- *½ chicken bouillon cube*
- *2 sprigs fresh coriander*

If Japanese shitake mushrooms are unavailable, substitute another variety of dried mushroom. Soften dried mushrooms in a little water before using.

Pasta with cèpes and black truffles

Ingredients

- *6 small cèpes*
- *2 tablespoons olive oil*
- *7 oz. (200 g) fresh pasta*
- *½ cup (10 cl) heavy cream*
- *1 teaspoon black truffle shavings*
- *¼ teaspoon crushed mixed peppercorns*
- *salt*
- *2 sprigs tarragon*

Wipe the cèpes carefully, first removing the earthy stems, and cut in half lengthwise. Pour 1 tablespoon olive oil in a nonstick frying pan over medium heat and sauté the cèpes, stirring to cook evenly. Set aside and keep warm. Cook the pasta according to the instructions on the packet in a large pot of boiling salted water, to which you have added 1 tablespoon olive oil. Pour the cream into the pan used for frying the cèpes. Add the truffle shavings, and season with the crushed mixed peppercorns and the salt. Reduce over a low heat for 5 minutes. Wash and drain the tarragon leaves. Drain the pasta and transfer to serving plates. Garnish with the cèpes and tarragon leaves, and pour over the sauce. Serve immediately.

You can vary this recipe using chanterelles, oyster mushrooms, or whatever other mushrooms are in season.

Cream of avocado with arugula and Tabasco

118

Ingredients

- *7 oz. (200 g) arugula*
- *1 avocado*
- *6 sprigs fresh coriander*
- *½ chicken bouillon cube*
- *juice of 1 lemon*
- *4 drops Tabasco*
- *¼ teaspoon crushed mixed peppercorns*
- *½ teaspoon kosher salt*
- *2 teaspoons crème fraîche*
- *2 teaspoons trout or salmon roe*

Blanch the arugula for 1 minute in boiling water, drain, and cool. Peel the avocado and remove the pit. Wash and drain the coriander leaves. Dissolve ½ chicken bouillon cube in ½ cup hot water. Pour into a blender bowl and add the arugula, avocado, coriander leaves, and lemon juice. Blend until creamy: if too thick, dilute with a little cold water. Season with the Tabasco, crushed mixed peppercorns, and kosher salt and put in the refrigerator to chill. To serve, pour the chilled avocado cream into small soup bowls, garnish with the crème fraîche, and top with the salmon roe.

The avocado for this recipe should be very ripe but not discolored.
Avocadoes tend to become discolored if stored with citrus fruit.

Fresh figs, bresaola, and mascarpone

Ingredients

- *2 fresh figs*
- *4 slices bresaola ham*
- *2 tablespoons mascarpone*
- *2 tablespoons olive oil*
- *chopped chives*
- *½ teaspoon crushed mixed peppercorns*

Wash and drain the figs. Divide into quarters without cutting through the base of the fruit. Place a slice of bresaola on a serving plate, top with a cut fig, and end with a second slice of bresaola. Do the same on a second plate. Garnish each serving with a tablespoon of mascarpone, then sprinkle on the chopped chives and crushed mixed peppercorns. Drizzle with olive oil and serve at once.

For a more substantial dish, use a large slice
of toasted country bread as a base for the other ingredients.

Goat-cheese surprise
with cherries and poppy seeds

Ingredients

- *6 large, ripe whiteheart cherries*
- *½ fresh soft goat cheese*
- *3 tablespoons poppy seeds*

Wash, drain, and pit the cherries. Mash the goat cheese with a fork. Cover each cherry with the cheese and roll gently in the palm of the hand to form a smooth ball. Dredge the cheese balls with the poppy seeds. Chill. At serving time, use a serrated knife to cut the balls in half. Serve immediately.

Assembling the ingredients for this recipe can be a little tricky.
Follow each step carefully, and be sure the goat cheese is
well chilled before you begin.

Tiny crab-and-asparagus custards

Ingredients

- 8 dwarf green asparagus, or 6 large green asparagus tips
- 2 sprigs chervil
- ¾ cup (20 cl) light cream
- ½ cup (10 cl) milk
- 3 eggs
- salt, pepper
- 1 small can crabmeat

Preheat oven to 350°F (180°C).

Wash the asparagus and poach in boiling salted water for 5 minutes. Drain on paper towel. Wash and drain the chervil, reserve 2 whole sprigs for the garnish, chop the rest. In a bowl, mix together the cream, milk, eggs, and chopped chervil. Season with salt and pepper. Drain the water from the can of crabmeat and divide the contents between two ovenproof porcelain ramekins, add the asparagus, then cover with the custard mixture. Put the ramekins in a pan of hot water (the water should come halfway up the sides of the ramekins) and bake until the point of a sharp knife inserted into the custard comes out clean; the timing will depend on how large the ramekins are. Garnish each ramekin with a sprig of chervil and serve.

Canned crabmeat works well in this recipe, but vacuum-packed fresh crabmeat is even better, if you can obtain it.
It contains less moisture and is more flavorful.

Crème brûlée with foie gras

Preheat oven to 300°F (150°C°).

   Prepare the custard for the crème brûlée by mixing the egg yolks and granulated sugar in a bowl, then beat in the milk, cream, and kosher salt. Crush the blanched peanuts and spread them in the bottom of two ovenproof porcelain ramekins. Arrange the slices of foie gras on top and cover with the custard mixture. Place the ramekins in a pan of hot water (the water should come halfway up the sides of the ramekins) and bake for 30 minutes. To check that they are done, insert the point of a sharp knife into the custard; it should come out clean. Cool, and then chill in the refrigerator for at least 1 hour. Preheat the broiler. Wash and drain the herbs, remove the leaves. Sprinkle the custards with the brown sugar and grill for 5 minutes under the broiler until they form a golden crust. Garnish with the herbs and serve immediately.

Ingredients

- *2 egg yolks*
- *3 tablespoons granulated sugar*
- *½ cup (10 cl) milk*
- *½ cup (125 g) crème fraîche*
- *¼ teaspoon kosher salt*
- *1 tablespoon shelled, blanched peanuts*
- *2 small slices foie gras*
- *chives*
- *2 sprigs chervil*
- *2 sprigs coriander*
- *2 sprigs flat parsley*
- *2 teaspoons brown sugar*

The ramekins of custard may be prepared the day before and stored in the refrigerator. All that needs to be done the next day is to sprinkle on the brown sugar.

Pineapple with Szechuan pepper

Ingredients

- 1 small pineapple
- juice of ½ lime
- 2 sprigs mint
- ½ teaspoon ground Szechuan pepper

Use a sharp serrated knife to halve the pineapple lengthwise, remove the hard central core, then cut the flesh away from the skin. Make a single cut down the center of one of the pineapple halves and draw several evenly spaced cuts across the flesh to divide it into squares. Stagger the squares in a pattern and moisten with the lime juice. Do the same with the other pineapple half. Wash, drain, and chop the mint leaves. Place each pineapple half on a serving plate, sprinkle with the Szechuan pepper, and garnish with the chopped mint leaves. Serve chilled.

There are many varieties of pineapple. Victoria pineapples from the island of Réunion, which are particularly sweet and fragrant, are ideal for this recipe.

Chocolate mousse with candied ginger

Ingredients

- 2 eggs
- 2 oz. (60 g) bitter chocolate
- 2 tablespoons unsalted butter
- 1 tablespoon confectioners' (icing) sugar
- 2 tablespoons candied ginger

Separate the egg yolks and whites. Melt the chocolate in a small double boiler over boiling water. Cut the butter into small pieces and add to the melted chocolate, then transfer the chocolate mixture to a large bowl, add the egg yolks and sugar, and stir in well. Whisk the egg whites until stiff and fold in gently. Fill two ramekins or small dishes with the mousse and chill for several hours in the refrigerator. Just before serving, chop the candied ginger and scatter over the mousses.

For best results, be sure to use a chocolate with a high cocoa content.

Springtime on the Terrace

These recipes call for young, astringent wines
such as Muscadet, Côteaux du Languedoc,
Irouléguy rosé, Cassis white, Tavel,
and young Spanish reds.

Large pasta shells with pesto and shrimp

Ingredients

- *4 conchiglioni*
- *(large pasta shells)*
- *7 oz. (200 g) cooked shrimp*
- *2 tablespoons pesto*
- *8 black olives*
- *2 sprigs basil*
- *4 tablespoons olive oil*

Cook the pasta for 15 minutes in a large pot of boiling salted water to which you have added 1 tablespoon olive oil. Rinse in cold water. Shell the shrimp, discarding the heads, and mix with the pesto. Fill the pasta shells with this stuffing. Pit and chop the olives, then wash and drain the basil leaves. Arrange the pasta shells on two serving plates, drizzle the rest of the olive oil over them, sprinkle with the chopped olives, and garnish with basil leaves. Serve immediately with 2 large slices of toasted country bread.

If you use frozen shelled shrimp for this recipe, be sure to drain the shrimp thoroughly first.

Cream of zucchini soup with tarragon

133

Wash and wipe the zucchini, trim the ends, and slice. Fill a pot with 1½ cups water, add the bouillon cube and bring to a boil before adding the sliced zucchini. Allow to cook for 15 minutes. Transfer everything to a blender, add the crème fraîche and crushed mixed peppercorns, and blend. Add salt and pepper to taste and pour into soup plates. Wash and drain the sprigs of tarragon and add as a garnish.

Ingredients

- *1 lb. (500 g) small zucchini*
- *1 chicken bouillon cube*
- *1 rounded tablespoon crème fraîche, or fresh goat cheese*
- *½ teaspoon crushed mixed peppercorns*
- *salt*
- *2 sprigs tarragon*

Choose zucchini that are small, firm, and a shiny deep green.

Monkfish skewers with bay leaf, olive oil, and chili powder

Ingredients

- *3 tablespoons olive oil*
- *½ teaspoon chili powder*
- *2 sprigs thyme*
- *1 lb. (450 g) boned monkfish*
- *6 small wooden skewers*
- *6 slices chorizo sausage*
- *6 bay leaves*
- *½ teaspoon crushed mixed peppercorns*

Pour the olive oil into a shallow ovenproof dish and add the chili powder and thyme leaves. Cut the monkfish into 6 chunks and add to the dish, making sure the pieces are coated well with the marinade. Chill for 1 hour in the refrigerator.

Preheat the oven to 400°F (200°C).

Thread the wooden skewers with a slice of chorizo sausage, a piece of fish, and a bay leaf each. Put the skewers back in the marinade dish and place in the oven to bake for about 10 minutes. Check frequently to see if they are ready. Immediately before serving the skewers, sprinkle them with the crushed mixed peppercorns.

Choose mild or spicy chorizo sausage, depending on personal taste. Try to find a homemade chorizo from a specialty foodstore if you can, as it will be firmer and easier to slice.

Three-color tapas

You'll need to prepare all the ingredients in advance and assemble the tapas just before serving. Drain the anchovy fillets on paper towel, cut the grilled peppers into julienne strips and moisten with olive oil, pit and chop the black olives. Use a vegetable parer to cut shavings of Parmesan cheese. Wash and prepare the herbs. Just before you are ready to eat, toast the slices of bread. Spread two slices with the tapenade, and garnish with the shredded Parmesan and basil leaves. Lay strips of grilled pepper on two more slices, and top with the chopped olives and some of the thyme leaves. Put the sun-dried tomatoes on the last two slices of toast, and top with the anchovy fillets and remaining thyme leaves. Serve immediately.

Ingredients
- *2 anchovy fillets in oil*
- *¼ yellow pepper, grilled*
- *¼ red pepper, grilled*
- *2 tablespoons olive oil*
- *4 black olives*
- *1 oz. (30 g) Parmesan cheese*
- *2 sprigs basil*
- *2 sprigs thyme*
- *6 thin slices of country bread, cut diagonally*
- *2 teaspoons tapenade (black-olive paste)*
- *2 sun-dried tomatoes*

Serve tapas as snacks with aperitifs; they can be made with almost anything you happen to have to hand.

Salmon carpaccio with pink peppercorns

Ingredients

- *10 oz. (300 g) salmon carpaccio*
- *3 tablespoons olive oil*
- *juice of 1 lemon*
- *1 teaspoon pink peppercorns*
- *2 sprigs dill*
- *½ teaspoon kosher salt*

Arrange the salmon carpaccio on two serving plates. Moisten with the olive oil and lemon juice, garnish with the pink peppercorns and dill leaves. At the last minute, sprinkle with kosher salt; serve with pieces of toast.

You can serve this as a main dish accompanied with new potatoes in salted butter.

Beef salad with lemongrass

Ingredients

- *5 oz. (150 g) angel hair or Chinese noodles*
- *10 oz. (300 g) cold roast beef*
- *1 lemongrass stalk*
- *piece of ginger root ¾ inch (2 cm) long*
- *2 sprigs coriander*
- *1 tablespoon sesame seeds*
- *juice of 1 lemon*
- *2 tablespoons sesame oil*
- *1 tablespoon soy sauce*
- *2 oz. (60 g) bean sprouts*

Cut the roast beef into thin slices. Cook the angel hair or Chinese noodles according to the directions on the packet, drain, and set aside to cool. Chop the lemongrass, peel and chop the ginger, wash, drain, and chop the coriander and bean sprouts. Brown the sesame seeds in an ungreased frying pan. Make a sauce by mixing together the lemon juice, soy sauce, and sesame oil with the chopped lemongrass, ginger, coriander, and sesame seeds. Heap the noodles on two serving plates and garnish with the beef slices and bean sprouts. Drizzle with the sauce and serve immediately.

You can use leftover roast pork, veal, or poultry in this recipe instead of beef; or vary the dish by adding tropical fruit.

Spring-vegetable tart

Preheat oven to 350°F (150°C).

 Wash and peel the carrots, turnips, and beans, steam for 10 minutes, and set aside. Wash and drain the salad leaves, chop the basil. Roll out the pastry and line a pie tin with it, trim the edge. Place a sheet of aluminum foil on top of the pastry shell and fill it with dried beans to prevent the pastry from rising. Bake for 15 minutes. Remove the pie tin from the oven, discard the dried beans and aluminum foil, and allow the pastry shell to cool. Wilt the green salad leaves with 1 tablespoon olive oil in a frying pan over medium heat, then put them in the pastry shell. Next, add 2 tablespoons olive oil and the granulated sugar to the frying pan, return to the heat, and sauté the steamed vegetables for 3 minutes. Lay them on top of the wilted leaves, garnish with the chopped basil, season with pepper and kosher salt, and serve immediately.

141

Ingredients

- *8 new carrots*
- *4 new turnips*
- *5 oz. (150 g) string beans*
- *5 oz. (150 g) mixed salad leaves*
- *1 sprig basil*
- *1 sheet ready-to-cook pastry*
- *3 tablespoons olive oil*
- *1 tablespoon granulated sugar*
- *¼ teaspoon ground pepper*
- *¼ teaspoon kosher salt*

If it's not the season for spring vegetables, you can use regular small vegetables, or cut larger ones into small pieces.

Green asparagus and Parmesan rolled in Parma ham

142

Ingredients

- 6 spears green asparagus
- 3 sprigs chervil
- a few chives
- ½ tablespoon balsamic vinegar
- 3 tablespoons olive oil
- ½ teaspoon crushed mixed peppercorns
- ½ teaspoon kosher salt
- 6 very thin slices Parma ham
- 1 oz. (30 g) grated Parmesan cheese

Cut the tough ends off the asparagus and cook the trimmed spears in a pot of boiling salted water for 10 minutes. Drain on paper towel and allow to cool. Continue to boil the water that the asparagus cooked in until it has reduced by one-half. Wash and drain the herbs. Prepare the vinaigrette by mixing together the balsamic vinegar, 2 tablespoons of olive oil, 2 tablespoons of the reduced cooking liquid, the crushed mixed peppercorns, kosher salt, and herbs. Place the grated Parmesan cheese on a plate. Brush the asparagus spears with the remaining olive oil, turn them over in the Parmesan cheese, and then roll up each spear in a slice of Parma ham. Arrange the rolls on the serving plates, and moisten with the herb vinaigrette. Serve immediately.

Vary the flavor of the vinaigrette with different seasonal herbs. You can also add a tablespoon of sesame seeds that have been browned for 1 minute in an ungreased frying pan.

Pork tenderloin with herb vinaigrette and baked potato puffs

Preheat oven to 400°F (200°C).

Wash and wipe the potatoes, cut in half lengthwise, and place skin-side down in a shallow ovenproof pan. Bake for 45 minutes; when done, the potatoes should be puffed and golden. Wash and wipe the tomato, cut in two, remove the seeds and solid core, chop into small dice. Wash and chop the basil leaves, peel and chop the shallot. Prepare the vinaigrette by mixing together the balsamic vinegar, olive oil, 1 tablespoon water, mustard, shallot, diced tomato, and chopped basil. Set aside. Trim, wash, and drain the lettuce. Set aside. Cut the pork tenderloin into thin slices. Beat the egg in a bowl with the flour. Spread the breadcrumbs on a plate. Heat the peanut oil in a frying pan. Dip the slices of pork in the beaten egg mixture and then in the breadcrumbs. Cook in the hot oil for about 10 minutes, turning once. When the pork is cooked, remove from the oil and drain on paper towel. Heap a mound of lettuce on two serving plates, top with the slices of pork, garnish with the potato puffs, and moisten with the vinaigrette, and serve.

Ingredients

- *6 small new potatoes*
- *1 large tomato*
- *2 sprigs basil*
- *1 shallot*
- *1 tablespoon balsamic vinegar*
- *2 tablespoons olive oil*
- *1 teaspoon Dijon mustard*
- *2 oz. (60 g) lettuce in season*
- *1 pork tenderloin, weighing about 1 lb. (450 g)*
- *1 egg*
- *2 tablespoons flour*
- *4 tablespoons breadcrumbs*
- *1 cup (25 cl) peanut oil*

145

For a more exotic touch, try substituting soy sauce for the balsamic vinegar.

Pink-grapefruit cocktail

Ingredients

- *1 pink grapefruit*
- *2 teaspoons brown sugar*
- *1 cup (25 cl) semi-sparkling (Italian) white wine, chilled*

Using a serrated knife, peel the grapefruit and gently detach the segments of fruit, removing all the pith. Place 1 teaspoon of brown sugar in each wine glass, top with a grapefruit segment, and fill the glasses with the wine. To develop the flavor, swirl the grapefruit sections in the wine before drinking.

This refreshing cocktail can also be made with good-quality sparkling wine.

Serves 2 | Preparation time: **15 minutes** | Cooking time: **30 minutes**

Cheese and hazelnut puffs

Ingredients

- *5 tablespoons butter*
- *½ cup (150 g) sifted flour*
- *4 eggs*
- *4 oz. (100 g) grated Comté cheese*
- *1 oz. (30 g) shelled, blanched hazelnuts*

Preheat oven to 400°F (200°C).

Place 1 cup (25 cl) water in a pot and bring to a boil. Add 4 tablespoons butter. Remove from the heat, add the flour, and beat until the mixture forms a smooth ball and begins to pull away from the sides of the pot. If the ball of dough seems too wet, place the pot over a low heat and beat for a few seconds longer. Away from the heat, add the eggs one by one, beating well after each addition. Beat in the grated cheese. Crush the blanched hazelnuts. Butter a baking sheet. Using a teaspoon, form the dough into small balls, place on the baking sheet, and dust with the crushed hazelnuts. Bake for 15–20 minutes, checking frequently. When done, the pastry balls will be puffed and golden. Serve warm for breakfast.

You can vary this recipe by adding herbs, whole grains, etc.
Comté cheese can be substituted with Gruyère.

148

Stuffed pears with red berries, pistachios, and pear liqueur

Ingredients

- ⅓ cup (100 g) granulated sugar
- 2 large ripe pears
- 2 oz. (60 g) red currants
- 2 oz. (60 g) strawberries
- 2 tablespoons pear liqueur
- 1 tablespoon shelled pistachios
- 2 sprigs mint

Make a syrup by boiling the sugar in 1½ cups water. Peel the pears, cut them in half lengthwise, and remove the stems and cores. Poach the pear halves in the sugar syrup for 10 minutes and allow to cool. Wash the red currants and strawberries, place in a small bowl with the pear liqueur, and chill in the refrigerator for 1 hour. Crush the pistachios. Arrange the pears on serving plates and fill the scooped-out centers with the marinated fruits. Mix the marinade with 2 tablespoons of the poaching syrup and pour over the pears. Before serving, sprinkle with the crushed pistachios.

The types of pear suitable for this recipe include Bartlett (Williams), Comice, Conference, Butter Pear, and Louise-Bonne.

Strawberry soup
with mascarpone and pink sugar

Ingredients

- *8 oz. (250 g) strawberries*
- *juice of ½ lemon*
- *2 teaspoons confectioners' (icing) sugar*
- *½ cup (125 g) mascarpone*
- *1 sprig mint*
- *1 teaspoon pink sugar*

Wash and drain the strawberries, remove the stems. Set four strawberries aside for the garnish. Combine the remaining strawberries with the lemon juice and confectioners' sugar. Using an electric beater or wire whisk, beat the mascarpone until firm. Transfer the strawberry mixture to parfait glasses, add the mascarpone, garnish with the whole strawberries, mint leaves, and pink sugar. Serve well chilled.

Use different types of strawberry, depending on the season. Compare the varieties available in your market before making your selection.

Index

Acknowledgments

Our thanks to Nathalie and Philippe for their gracious welcome, and for allowing us to use their house and garden as the background for the photographs contained in this book.

Cocooning
China: Catherine Memmi, rue Saint-Sulpice, 75006 Paris, France
Tablecloth: Reine de France, tel: +33 (0)2 43 71 54 82
Tableware: Siècle, 24 rue du Bac, 75007 Paris, France
Lamp globes, coffee cups: L'Atelier Couleurs, La Coispillère, 61260 Ceton, France

Dinner by Candlelight
Tablecloth: Reine de France, tel: +33 (0)2 43 71 54 82
China: Bernardaud, rue Royale, 75008 Paris, France
Glasses, tableware: Siècle, 27 rue du Bac, 75007 Paris, France

In the Kitchen
China: Palais-Royal, 12 rue des Quatre Vents, 75006 Paris, France

A Riverside Lunch
China: Catherine Memmi, rue Saint-Sulpice, 75006 Paris, France
Glasses, teapot, tableware: L'Atelier Couleurs, La Coispillère, 61260 Ceton, France

Bedside Dinners
Embroidered bedcovering: Reine de France, tel: +33 (0)2 43 71 54 82
China: Palais Royal, 12 rue des Quatre Vents, 75006 Paris, France
Tray, glasses, tableware: L'Atelier Couleurs, La Coispillère, 61260 Ceton, France

Springtime on the Terrace
China, place mats, glasses, tableware, napkins: L'Atelier Couleurs, La Coispillère, 61260 Ceton, France